Living Stress-Free

An Abundant Life Bible Study

by Tracy Wainwright

TLC Wainwright Publishing, LLC
VIRGINIA

Living Stress-Free

an Abundant Life Bible Study

Copyright © 2015 by Tracy L. Wainwright
          Published by TLC Wainwright Publishing, LLC
          P.O. Box 1001
          Toano, VA 23168

All rights reserved. No part of this book may be reproduced, scanned, or distributed in any printed form or by any electronic or mechanical means, including information storage or retrieval systems, without permission in writing from the publisher, except by a reviewer who may quote brief passages in a review.

Unless otherwise indicated, all Scripture quotations are taken from the Holy Bible, New Living Translation, copyright © 1996, 2004, 2007 by Tyndale House Foundation. Used by permission of Tyndale House Publishers, Inc., Carol Stream, Illinois 60188. All rights reserved.

Scripture quotations marked {AMP} are taken from the Amplified® Bible, Copyright © 2015 by The Lockman Foundation. Used by permission." (www.Lockman.org)

Scripture quotations marked {KJV} are taken from the Authorized (King James) Version. Rights in the Authorized Version in the United Kingdom are vested in the Crown. Reproduced by permission of the Crown's patentee, Cambridge University Press.

Scripture quotations marked {MSG} are taken from *The Message*. Copyright © 1993, 1994, 1995, 1996, 2000, 2001, 2002. Used by permission of NavPress Publishing Group.

Cover Photo taken by Tracy Wainwright

Cover design by Rachel Piferi

ISBN-10: 0989948544
ISMB-13: 978-0-9899485-4-8

Contents

Week 1	Evaluating & Surrendering	1
Week 2	Overloaded Calendars	27
Week 3	Relationships	57
Week 4	Situations & Circumstances	89
About the Author		121

O L̲ord̲, you are righteous,
and your regulations are fair.
Your laws are perfect
and completely trustworthy.
I am overwhelmed with indignation,
for my enemies have disregarded your words.
Your promises have been thoroughly tested;
that is why I love them so much.
I am insignificant and despised,
but I don't forget your commandments.
Your justice is eternal,
and your instructions are perfectly true.
As pressure and stress bear down on me,
I find joy in your commands.
Your laws are always right;
help me to understand them so I may live.
Psalm 119:137-144
{emphasis added}

Week 1
Evaluating & Surrendering

Section 1

Stress is a part of life. Have you noticed that? Everyone seems stressed these days. In a world where we have access to just about any information we want and have conveniences and helps to do our work in life more than any other time in history, we are more stressed than ever.

I haven't taken any polls or researched the statistics to come to these conclusions, but simply observed life. Both my life and the lives of others.

A brief online search on "how to eliminate stress" brings up over 8,000,000 results. Yes, that's 8 million! Obviously people are looking for ways to eliminate stress.

Under the results are topics like "How to Reduce Stress," "Stress Management," "Ways to Relieve Stress," and "Natural Ways to Fight Stress." I'm sure all of these websites have some great tips, tricks, and tools, but I didn't go read them all. First, I didn't want to stress myself out with an overload of information. Second, I really want this book to have something new. This is to be completely and totally biblically grounded and led by the Spirit.

By the way, a brief search on Amazon also shows the great hunger people have for dealing with stress. A search in books for "stress" provided over 58,000 results, with almost 5,000 in Religion and Spirituality.

There are a lot of resources out there! So why should you pick this one?

Because it doesn't just offer pat answers or strategies. It offers insight to biblical wisdom that will *radically change your life*.

While we can do lots of things in this world to eliminate, alleviate, and handle stress better, God and His Word always offer wisdom that goes beyond what we can come up with or implement ourselves. It also lends to having external and eternal impacts, instead of just an internal impact most resources offer.

The goal is not to just offer you a way to live stress-free, but how to live in abundant peace – the complete opposite of living stressed.

Check-in Time
What is your stress level today? (circle or mark with X)

1	2	3	4	5
at peace	a little stressed	a lot's going on	somewhat overwhelmed	not sure how I'm getting out of bed

What is causing you stress right now? (There's a spot to write down your thoughts, but don't rush through this part or skip something just because you don't want to write it down. Really consider the things in your life that add stress – good or bad: a major life change, health situation, job, schedule, relationship, family member, etc.)

_____

_____

_____

Now, categorize these sources of stress. Because there are somethings that we have control over and some that are completely out of control, it's important before we start looking at how we reduce or manage stress to examine how much is within our control.

Stressors that I can change now:
_____
_____

Stressors that I can change later:
_____
_____

Stressors that I cannot change:
_____
_____

Great job! It's not always easy doing self-examination. Actually, it's usually the hardest part. The whole concept of you can't change what you don't acknowledge.

Which may lead you to think that our next step is to start changing some of these things. We're not ready to go there yet, though. First, we must do the real first step.

As you end this section of the Bible study, I'm going to recommend that you take some time to pray. Pray over these items that you've listed. Pray over the items you didn't feel comfortable writing down. Pray that God will reveal anything that you haven't yet thought of.

As you pray, really seek to offer each one of these - situations, relationships, events - up to the Lord. Don't yet ask Him for guidance, clarity, or answers. Just offer them up to Him.

Lay them in His hands. Trust Him with each and every one of them.

Then ask Him for strength to trust that He will guide you, when you get to that point, in every single detail of every single item.

~~~*~~~
The LORD directs the steps of the godly,
He delights in every detail of their lives.
Psalm 37:23
~~~*~~~

Section 2

I wish we could sit down over a cup of coffee (decaf for me!) and talk about what God revealed to you in your prayer time. Or maybe He didn't reveal anything to you, but gave you a bit more peace or knowing that you're not in this all alone.

I pray that your time of prayer was sweet, and you are feeling the freedom of laying things at the feet of Jesus.

Maybe you started today just as stressed as the day before. Maybe you woke up and life started coming at you at breakneck speed. Maybe you're so used to carrying everything that you picked it all right back up. That's okay! This is not a quick, one-shot, aiming at perfection deal. No, this is a process seeking progress. One step at a time. One day at a time.

The first steps are to be real and acknowledge that we all have stress in our lives. I guess we're a little backwards though, because we did the second first. Now we're going to do the first second.

And once you've figured that out, we'll move forward.

We've acknowledged our stressors. We've also prayed over them. Not in an I'm-ready-for-an-answer/solution kind of way. But an It's-all-yours-Jesus way.

I said praying about our stressors in life was the first step, but by no means is it the last. This is just the beginning of the process.

However, even though we're going to walk through changing how these events, relationships and situations affect us, we will not pick them back up.

Okay, so we've probably already picked some, if not all, of them back up already, but that's not the goal. The goal is to continually submit them to the Lord.

As we do that, let's get real with each other.

We know that different things in life cause different levels of stress. No matter what the level of stress is though, how we handle it is of utmost importance.

My stressors aren't more important than yours and you're aren't more important than mine. They all affect our lives, our outlooks, and our emotional health. They also affect our relationship with the Lord, with ourselves, and with others.

The list could go on. These things impact us, or they wouldn't be a source of stress.

These can be things we consider little. Or things considered huge.

They could be:
- A move
- A new job
- A new family member
- Marriage
- Divorce
- An unhealthy friend or family member
- A friend or family member with mental health issues
- Depression
- Chronic pain

- Chronic illness
- A physical assault
- Emotional assaults
- A loved one injured in an accident
- Death of a loved one
- A schedule that's overflowing with way too many things on it
- A house full of young children
- A sticky situation at work, home, or church
- A difficult living situation
- Sexual molestation/assault on you or a loved one

This list, too, could go on. Some of these stressors are just a part of life. Some of them go beyond the everyday ups and downs.

We live in a fallen, sick, sinful world. The results of that are many of the things listed above.

We should not be surprised when difficulties come.

Jesus warned us we would have trouble here on earth.

Look up John 16:33 and write it on the lines below:

_____

_____

_____

_____

_____

Troubles are not unexpected – not if we acknowledge the world we live in.

Yet we live in a culture that tells us every bad thing can be prevented. This sets us up for great disappointment, heartache, and an inability to handle the hard, difficult, and tragic things that come along.

BUT GOD. Jesus was not surprised by evil and tragedy. Saddened, yes. Heartbroken, yes. Compassionate, yes. He was never, however, caught off guard nor did He allow anything to steal His peace.

Because He was the very essence of God (Philippians 2:6; Hebrews 1:3; Colossians 2:9). He embodied the nature of God, which includes a peace that transcends evil.

Look back at John 16:33. Not only did Jesus forewarn us of these troubles that would be a part of life, but He also provided an answer: He has given us knowledge through His words – His direction to abide in Him, remain in His love, to expect hatred from the world, that He was sending the Spirit of truth to us to comfort and guide us, that we will see Him one day and have ultimate joy that can't be taken from us, and that He has overcome the world and all its sorrows.

> *Read John 15-16 for an in depth look at these concepts and to multiply the blessings that come from reading the Word.

Jesus has given us His very Spirit, and one of the blessings that comes along with it is peace in Him.

As we continue in this study, we'll look deeper into how peace is the opposite of stress and how we can start tapping into this unlimited resource more effectively.

Are you ready to trade in stress for peace?

Today, let's pray for a greater understanding of God's peace. Ask Him to reveal Himself and what His Spirit dwelling in you means on a deeper level. Seek spiritual wisdom and understanding.

~~~*~~~
We ask God to give you complete
knowledge of his will and to give you
spiritual wisdom and understanding.
Colossians 1:9b
~~~*~~~

Section 3

When I think of peace, I picture a hammock gently swaying in the breeze, or a deserted beach with waves softly crashing, or being curled up in a cozy recliner with a cup of steaming coffee.

What do you think of when you ponder the concept of peace?

_____

_____

Did you notice the similarities in all of these images related to peace? They are all situational.

Even I tend to view peace from the outside instead of something to be harnessed and lived out from within.

There is nothing wrong with all of these scenarios, but they are few and far between. If we are to live a life of peace we have two options:

- (1) Leave everything and everyone behind and live on a deserted island which hopefully has abundant food and no predatory animals.
- (2) Learn how to embrace and be filled with the peace of the Lord which "surpasses understanding."

Since for 99.99% of us option one isn't really an option, let's look at option two.

Before we seek to figure out how to do this for ourselves, let me share some examples with you.

The first is one of the most loving, caring, peaceful women I've ever met in my life. I met her when she was in her 60's and she was a darling woman. The way that she exuded joy, love, and peace, I would have thought that everything in life had always gone her way. That she was tremendously blessed of the Lord.

The second part of that assumption was true. She was greatly blessed by the Lord. Life had not, however, always gone her way.

This precious woman and her husband had one child, whom they had late in life. Anyone who's struggled with fertility or known a loved one who has can imagine the years and years of struggle before their child entered their life.

Her challenges weren't all in the past, however. She also suffered Hepatitis A, contracted when she needed a blood transfusion to save her life decades before.

She never complained. She never wined. She never proclaimed her situation wasn't fair. Not even when death approached.

Her joy remained. Her peace remained. She still proclaimed the glory of the Lord.

Since you may be thinking that at least she lead a long, fruitful life and that may be the source of her peace, let me share about another woman.

This one was in her early thirties when she lost her battle with cancer. A battle she had fought for over ten years.

Despite powerful, life-altering treatments and surgeries, despite knowing she'd never see her child grow up or grow old with her husband, despite facing death decades before most people, she was full of peace.

She was grateful for every blessing she had and every day she was able to take a breath and love her child. She proclaimed God's faithfulness to every promise He'd ever made. As a matter of fact, she rejoiced that He'd exceeded many of His promises.

Even facing certain death, while she prepared her child to lose his mother, she was at peace. She had firmly placed her trust in Jesus not only as Savior, but also as Lord of every single detail of her life.

Can you imagine facing great struggles and having perfect calm? Can you picture dealing with daily challenges without losing peace?

It is possible. To have stressors in our lives, yet not let stress rule and reign in our lives.

We know that this peace comes from the Lord, but it often seems the most difficult thing is to get it from our heads into our hearts.

How do we grasp, integrate, and live in God's peace?

First, which is what I believe the two ladies referenced previously had, is an *eternal focus*. They kept their eyes fixed on forever life in heaven, not the temporary life we live here on earth.

They seemed to understand what Paul says in Romans

8:18 – "Yet what we suffer now is nothing compared to the glory he will revel to us later."

You may be thinking: "You don't know my situation" or "I've tried that, it didn't work."

I get it, there are circumstances and relationships that seem to take over our lives, or are so devastating we can't possibly take our focus off them.

Or so we think.

    But it is possible.

        It takes faith.

           It takes trust.

              It takes surrender.

We started the process on day 1, but will continue it as we dig deeper over the next few days and weeks.

Check-in Time
What is the *one thing* that is causing you the most stress right now?

_____

How long has that one thing been an issue?

_____

Is this one thing something you can effect a change on or is it completely out of your control?

_____

Are you willing to surrender this *one thing* to Jesus? Not ask Him to change it, or reveal an answer/solution to you, but just to surrender it.

Admit that He is Lord even over this. That nothing, not even this, happens outside His sovereignty and power.

Lift this one thing up to Him in prayer today. Cry out to Him. Seek His face and presence in the midst of this one thing. Ask Him to strengthen you to let it go. Not that it's not still a concern or a reality, but to change your focus around this one thing so that you can see past it to the hope He has given us of eternal glory with Him.

Digging Deeper: Pick a word and do a Bible search. Use the space below or a journal to record some of the scriptures you find. (This is easily done using a concordance book or website, such as www.biblegateway.com)

Words to pick from:

   (1) Faith
   (2) Trust
   (3) Humble

_____
_____
_____
_____
_____

~~~*~~~
Don't worry about anything; instead,
pray about everything. Tell God what you
need, and thank him for all he has done.
Then you will experience God's peace,
which exceeds anything you can understand.
His peace will guard your hearts and minds
as you live in Christ Jesus.
Philippians 4:6-7
~~~*~~~

Section 4

I wonder if we're going too slow. Yet I know my tendency is to race through things and just look forward to the next thing. It's a lot easier to ignore things and keep moving forward.

That is the temptation on day four of our study. I don't want to lose you. I don't want you to get restless or bored or distracted.

Yet, when I think about moving to the next step towards a stress-free life, I know that it is not time yet. We must pause and rest where we are.

I know this. And God recently reinforced this in me.

I do have a tendency to tuck my head and keep pushing forward, somewhat like you would in a downpouring of rain. I don't get any less wet. All I'm really doing is shielding my face from the brunt onslaught.

I am the same way with life sometimes. I just keep moving forward, not stopping to acknowledge what's going on, how it's impacting me, or how I'm dealing with it – or as the case often is, how I'm *not* dealing with it.

How do you usually react to stressful situations or relationships?

_____

_____

_____

_____

I don't believe ignoring stressors is the right way to handle them, nor biblical. God did not create us as ostriches. Our heads are not meant to be buried in the sand.

Nor is it biblical to worry and fret over stressful things in our lives.

It's interesting to me that God has allowed this past year leading up to teaching a session and writing a Bible study on living stress-free be one of the most stressful years I've had in a long time. Maybe He wanted me to learn the lessons first hand and have a chance to put them into practice?

I won't go into vivid details, because the details of stressful situations aren't important to the discussion. There are some of you who'll read the synopsis and think, "Oh my goodness, what a year!" Others of you will think, "Well, that was nothing compared to what I've been through."

Remember, it's not in the comparison that we find peace and comfort and deal better with our situation. But I will still share the overview, so you can understand that I understand. This past year wasn't the most stressful I've ever had, but God has certainly used some challenging situations to teach me how to rest in His peace rather than rely on myself to "fix" everything (often the source of great stress – the idea that we hold responsibility on more than we really do; but more on that later.)

So, in the past year my husband and I decided to buy a piece of property to build on. We had a verbal contract and were waiting on some other things to come together before completing the written contract. We started getting our house ready for the market. Then we saw evidence that the deal was going sideways. Someone had come in to buy it out from under us.

For weeks I stressed. It was affecting my mood, my health, and outlook. I begged, pleaded, and bargained with God to work it out in our favor. Then one day, I finally stopped and listened to God. He reassured me that He had heard my cries and He would do what was in the best interest of me and my family.

I decided to trust Him and stop stressing.

Yes, I just decided. And the next day I noticed dramatic changes in my health and attitude. A short time later it was confirmed that "our" piece of property was being sold to someone else.

I was okay with it. Because I knew I wasn't in charge. God was.

Since we had our house ready to go on the market, we decided to see if there was another property that fit what we wanted. We found one that was just as close, but better.

God is so good and His knowledge, plans, and ways are so much better than ours.

From the day we signed that written contract, this is what followed: 6 weeks later we had a contract on our house, 8 weeks later we closed on the property, and 13 weeks later we moved in with my in-laws to prepare to build.

Then the plans began to take forever. Where I thought we'd be breaking ground within two months, at over four months the plans weren't even ready to submit.
Again I began to stress. My family of 6 was, after all, living with my in-laws (who are great, but still come with challenges) in a three-bedroom house.

Then again I got quiet enough to listen to God. His message to me was again that my timeline and plans were not of utmost importance. His are.

I share bits of the recent part of my story so that you can see – so you can imagine – the stressors that have been a part of my life over the last year. But also so you can see how when we pause and really listen to God, how He answers faithfully.

That's why we're starting this study on living stress-free by surrendering and listening. These are key to prohibiting stressors in our lives from ruling and taking over.

We are able to not be overcome by stress when we have stressors in our lives because we know the God Most High, the Lord Almighty, the One whose perfect love never ends.

Look up and write out 1 John 4:16-18

_____

_____

_____

_____

_____

_____

_____

_____

_____

_____

_____

As we close out today, ask God to reveal to you the areas in which you haven't been willing to trust Him completely. Ask Him to reveal Himself to you in new ways. To remind you of His faithfulness, love, and grace. To bring to mind that He has it all – every single detail – under His Sovereignty. Ask Him to help you let go, truly loosen your grip of control (which is an illusion, anyway) and release the situations, events, and people to Him to do a mighty work that only He can do.

~~~*~~~
Rejoice in our confident hope.
Be patient in trouble,
and keep on praying.
Romans 12:12
~~~*~~~

Section 5

It's interesting to me that when I looked up the word "stress" on dictionary.com, I had to go to the third section of the definition (the 15th actual definition) to get the one I was thinking about: to worry.

The rest of the definitions focused on stress as in to emphasize, put pressure on, or strain. All of these definitions come before worry. However, I think I hit on something.

What is worry other than to put emphasis on something?

And what is stress other than our worry – rehearsing what has or could go wrong in any given situation?

We've talked about stressors and stress and how they are different. We all have stressors in our lives, albeit to different levels and degrees, but not everyone lives in a state of stress.

What's the difference between people who lived stressed and people who live stress-free, given the amount of stressors does not seem to make the difference?

Perspective and focus.

Most of us are familiar with the following verses, but have you ever thought of them in relation to the things that bring stress to your life?

> Therefore, since we are surrounded
> by such a huge crowd of witnesses
> to the life of faith, let us strip off
> every weight that slows us down,
> especially the sin that so easily trips us
> up. And let us run with endurance the
> race God has set before us. We do this
> by keeping our eyes on Jesus, the
> champion who initiates and perfects our
> faith. Because of the joy awaiting him, he
> endured the cross, disregarding its shame.
> Now he is seated in the place of
> honor beside God's throne.
> Hebrews 12:1-2

We know these verses call us to throw off sin, but have you ever thought of the other things that it references to that entangle us? I'd wager that stress is a major one of those entangling things today.

Stress wraps itself around your brain and heart and keeps you focused on the situation, event, or relationship. It has you rehash over and over what happened, what you could have done differently, and/or trying to reason why it happened. It has you mull over, meditate on, and mention repeatedly negative relationships and events. It has you wonder, fret over, and try to figure out what you can do to produce good outcomes and prevent negative ones in the future. It has you focus on the bad, the ugly, and yourself. It winds its tentacles around you to the extent that your feet are bound, keeping you from living an abundant, effective, fruitful life for the Lord.

And yes, worry is sin.

It entangles your life and prevents you from living with an eternal focus and bringing great glory to God.

How do you react to this statement: Worry is sin?

_____

_____

_____

_____

_____

How do we know worry and stress are sin?

Because the Bible tells us it is the opposite of faith:

> Brethren, for this reason, in [spite of all] our stress and crushing difficulties we have been filled with comfort and cheer about you [because of] your faith (the leaning of your whole personality on God in complete trust and confidence).
> 1 Thessalonians 3:5 (AMP)

> The seed that fell among the thorns represents others who hear God's word, but all too quickly the message is crowded out by the worries of this life, the lure of wealth, and the desire for other things, so no fruit is produced.
> Mark 4:18-19

Matthew 6:25-31 says "don't worry" four times. The

reason why? Because we are "far more valuable" to God than the birds, lilies of the field, or anything else in creation. God knows all of and will take care of every one of our needs. Our job is to seek His kingdom and live righteously. To keep our focus on Him.

We will continue to dig into scripture and talk about what to do instead of worry and stress, but I think it's important to first talk about what is not the opposite of a stress-controlled life.

Fixing our eyes on Jesus and keeping our minds fixed on the hope of God's glory and our rewards in heaven do not mean:

- We do not grieve, mourn, cry, get depressed, experience great pain
- We do not acknowledge painful situations, experiences, and relationships
- We ignore difficulties, challenges, and trials
- We don't feel the full weight of trauma, changes, and the unknown.

Choosing to focus on Jesus, His Word, and His truth, leaning and relying on Him, and trusting Him with everything *does not* mean we don't suffer. It just changes the way we suffer.

We feel the full force of the emotions that go along with leaving a long-time home, losing a child, having a spouse walk away, losing a job, surviving a trauma, etc. We simply are willing to trust the Lord with these details. That while they are not in His perfect will, they are in His sovereign will, and He will work it out for His glory and our good. *If we continue to love and trust Him.*

And as we just saw, stress and worry are the opposite of this type of faith.

As we close out week one, I don't want us to worry about how much we've worried – in the past or even today. Instead, let's choose to thank and praise the Lord for His grace and mercy to help us from this day forward to commit all of our stressors to Him and not try to hold onto or control them ourselves.

Let's commit to meditate on His Word instead of our worries.

Let's commit to throwing off EVERYTHING that hinders our walk with Jesus – because He has so much more in store for us!

These are our prayers for today – and hopefully every day as we move forward.

~~~*~~~
I pray that God, the source of hope,
will fill you completely with joy and
peace because you trust in him. Then
you will overflow with confident hope
through the power of the Holy Spirit.
Romans 15:13
~~~*~~~

Week 1 Group Discussion Questions

(1) How would you describe the difference between stressors in life and living stressed?

(2) What is the hardest thing for you to lay at the feet of Jesus and **really** trust Him with?

(3) Have your prayers surrounding the stressful things in your life changed over the last week? If so, how?

(4) In what ways should our relationship with Jesus change the way we view, handle, approach stressors in our lives?

(5) Discuss how you felt/feel about this statement: "Worry is sin."

(6) Why can we live joyfully despite the stressors in our lives? How would you explain it to someone else?

(7) Give an example of what God is teaching you – specifically about stressors in your life – through this study.

(8) If you were to pick one scripture that had the most impact from this week of study, which one would it be and why?

Week 2
Overcrowded Calendars

Section 1

As we move forward in pursuing a stress-free life, we'll take this week to talk about things that we have control over. We touched briefly on these things last week, but will now go in depth. We're tackling these first, because there are some active things we can do.

While prayer is always the first and best work, God also often calls us to action. The act of laying down our will and the details in our lives is action in our minds, but there is also action we can take physically.

On the surface, many of these options and changes seem easier. However, don't be surprised if your flesh revolts and those around you balk a little. After all, we cannot change without affecting change in those around us.

Our hope is, as we seek to change things in order to draw closer to Jesus and the life He desires for us to live, we'll recognize that the temporal changes, while challenging in the short run, will be beneficial for everyone in the long run.

Some people in our lives will see the long term benefits. Others won't. That may be one of the biggest challenges. But I want you to be encouraged, that if you are pursuing God and walking in obedience to Him, He will work it all out. Maybe not in our timing or the way we would have desired, but He will in His infinite wisdom and love.

Just as losing weight, earning a degree, raising God-fearing/loving children, or working toward just about any goal requires short-term sacrifice for long-term reward, so does living stress-free.

We have created lives that are full. However, much of the time they are full of things that add to our stress instead of relieve it. We are full of busyness, not necessarily full of fruitful work.

That's why we're going to attack, um examine, our schedules first.

Have you looked at your calendar lately? Have you felt the effects of racecar pace living? Have you found yourself lamenting how many obligations, activities, and events your family is involved in?

If not, let me invite you to contact me and tell me how in the world you managed to avoid it!

If you have, however, keep reading this section.

Earlier, I introduced the idea that while we have more conveniences than ever to rescue us from and reduce the amount of work it takes to live day-to-day, we have unlimited possibilities around us and in our lives that have filled those spaces 'til they are bursting at the seams.

The truth is, we are (in general) busier today than ever before. There are work things, fun things, athletic things, church things, friend things, family things, entertainment things, volunteer things, and relaxation things. Most of these aren't bad things – they in and of themselves aren't detrimental – but the sheer number of them can be overwhelming.

And they are crowding out Jesus. They are pushing Him to the side, to a corner, and in a box.

We're going to look at the seeds and weeds passage again, but this time from the Message Bible and a slightly different perspective.

> The seed cast in the weeds represents the ones who hear the kingdom news but are overwhelmed with worries about all the things they have to do and all the things they want to get. The stress strangles what they heard, and nothing comes of it.
> Mark 4:18-19 {MSG}

Let's focus on two phrases:

(1) They are "overwhelmed with worries about all the things they have to do and all the things they want to get."
(2) "The stress strangles what they heard, and nothing comes of it."

Have you ever felt overwhelmed with the worries of your to-do list, calendar obligations, and things you desired to obtain?

Think about that time (whether it was long ago, in the recent past, or you are there now). Where, in all of the worries, responsibilities, and commitments was Jesus in your life? Did you feel close to Him? Far from Him? Even know He was still there? Really stop and seek God to reveal how these things have crowded Him out of your mind and heart.

Below (or in a journal), write what the Lord reveals to you and your repentance from letting the things of this world shove Him out of His rightful place in your life.

_____

_____

_____

_____

_____

It's hard to face, but we often opt for stress in our lives instead of the King of Peace. All those fun, useful, helpful things are perishing.

Our hearts, are too often dedicated to the things of this word – even things that cause stress in our lives – rather than those things with eternal value.

Look up and write out Matthew 6:19-21

_____

_____

_____

_____

_____

_____

_____

_____

_____

_____

_____

Many of us are familiar with these verses, but I wonder how often we apply them to our lives.

As we ponder that, I'd like to share a story that might be somewhat familiar to you.

When my four children were little (they are 6-12 at this writing; yes, you calculated right that I had four children under 8 for a LONG time. Okay, three years isn't that long, but many days it felt that way. I digress...), I left the house with them all voluntarily on very rare occasions. When everyone hit the milestone of over 3, I began showing my (still bare of makeup) face in public again.

On one of these outings, we all went to an amusement park. With friends (I still wasn't brave enough to go alone). It was a lot of work. I packed a bag with diapers, snacks, drinks, extra clothes, towels, passes, the camera, and other odds and ends mothers of young children don't leave home without.

We loaded the car, drove there, traipsed everyone across the parking lot, then through the park to hit all the fun spots.

By the end of the day I was exhausted. Fortunately none of my kids had thrown tantrums or lost it during our trip (I never went for a full day to help limit the chances of overload), but I had certainly seen plenty of it.

The thought struck me: Have we all gone crazy? We spend hundreds of dollars, lots of time, and walk until our legs are aching – to entertain our children who often end up massively grumpy at the end of the day.

Yes, I think we are. We are a bit cracked.

Now, don't get me wrong. We have gone back many times. It's much easier now. I don't think having fun is wrong. The question is, how many times do we sacrifice our peace and sanity for a bit of fun or entertainment?

In instances like the one I shared above – and in life.

Are you willing to look at your calendar, commitments, and activities?

Take some time. List them all. Yes, all of them. Yours, your spouse's, your children's. Break out the calendar (or calendars) and really examine them.

Then pray over them. Don't decide to do anything yet. Don't make drastic, impulsive changes. Really seek the Lord's will in each one.

We'll focus on these things this week, but don't feel like you even have to make the changes in that time span.

Let the Lord lead you. He knows so much more than we do and can direct us better than we can ourselves.

So for now, just pray. Lift each item up and then lay it down.

~~~*~~~
Trust in the LORD with all your heart;
do not depend on your own understanding.
Seek his will in all you do,
and he will show you which path to take.
Proverbs 3:5-6
~~~*~~~

Section 2

Today we're going to go back a little and dig in deeper to part of Mark 4:18 {MSG}.

> They are "overwhelmed with worries about all the things they have to do..."

Have you ever thought about how much the things in this life we have to do and want push God to the side?

I have. I've recognized it. Yet I still struggle to eliminate, reorganize, and structure things from my life so that God always comes first. It seems my flesh always gets in the way.

As I'm writing this, it's that time of year when school is about to begin. Extra-curricular activities are being signed up for. And the calendar is getting full.

It can be overwhelming. Cause stress. Take over our peace and focus from the Lord.

Besides removing ourselves from life, what can we do to make sure the things we have to do don't overwhelm us?

What tactics have you learned to prevent becoming overwhelmed?

_____
_____
_____
_____

I hope you've seen a strong theme throughout this study so far – prayer. Prayer and knowing God intimately enough to hear and heed His guidance are keys to not becoming overwhelmed.

First, and we've already started doing this in week 1, we pray over our commitments and obligations. We ask God to reveal what in our lives could be, and possibly should be, let go.

So far, we've only prayed over these things. Now it's time to take action.

In yesterday's lesson, we listed all of our obligations, responsibilities, activities, etc. We've prayed over it once. We're going to pray over it again, but with a heart to listen to God's guidance on what might need to go.

Take a few moments to pray over your list. Ask God to reveal to you what might need to be eliminated. Open yourself to WHATEVER He may say. It may not be what you think. It may catch you completely off guard. Or it may be what you've had an inkling of for some time now. Also, ask God what He wants you to keep and what you might need to adjust a bit. There is more than one option here. Lift it up to Him, then move on to the section below.

I hope you've had time to sit with the Lord and see the next step or two in how He'd like to rearrange your life. Maybe your activities, responsibilities, and commitments are already in balance and He didn't lead you to eliminate anything. Maybe He surprised you or confirmed what you've been feeling for a long time. Maybe He is blasting away the things that are crowding your calendar.

Regardless of what He's shown you, I hope that you will step out in faith and obey.

I'm a visual person. So when I have a list like this and get revelation about making changes I like to mark them somehow. Maybe you'll cross through the items that need to go. Maybe you star the things that need to change. Maybe you circle the things that remain unchanged. I invite you to mark your list, or maybe rewrite it under the two or three categories.

Got it done? Good! Now you plan. Some things can't be eliminated immediately. Some affect other people and you'll want to let them know the changes that are coming. Some you may want to discuss with your spouse or children and engage them in prayer, too.

The last thing you want to do is rush into changes that may hurt your integrity as someone who doesn't follow through or is untrustworthy. Working on changing how we live our lives and commit ourselves day-to-day takes time and transition.

Don't let the change stress you. It will be uncomfortable. Some changes will be more difficult than others. However, if it's something that's crowding God and His work out of our lives, we will be rewarded greatly by letting go.

I experienced this very thing recently. God had been leading me to be still and listen for months. I knew something on my list of responsibilities/ministries needed to go. I had no idea what, though. I loved everything I was doing. It was all "good" stuff.

As I prayed, God revealed the first thing pretty quickly. I wasn't that surprised. I hadn't prayed a bit about taking this task on. I enjoyed it, but it was taking away time I'd worked hard to create.

Then God revealed another item to me. This was only slightly a surprise. I'm still working on letting it go completely. I'm trying to transition it to another leader, but have let those in charge know that I'd be disobedient if I remained in the position.

Next came two more items that were a great surprise to me. I'd been working in these ministries for several years and they were where my heart was. However, God was clear. Those areas weren't where He wanted me serving right now.

After prayer and consideration, I put my notice in to both of the leaders I was serving under. I didn't quit. I gave my resignation for a couple months out.

It was hard to give up these ministries. One I'm still looking for a replacement for. (Praying about, seeking.) However, within a week of stepping out in this uncomfortable obedience, I received something I'd been waiting ten years on – my first book contract with a traditional publisher.

The publisher had held my manuscript for almost a year, and really should have gotten back with me months earlier. But God orchestrated the timing and events to show me that He rewards obedience.

I'm wondering if anyone's asking if God really cares about all these things. Does He really want to be involved in what ministries, extracurricular activities, and events we involve ourselves in?

The answer is a resounding YES!

He has given us every moment and every breath to live on this earth to glorify Him and share His grace and love with others. When we are too busy entertaining, training, or even working and serving to walk intimately with Him, He cares.

It's the moments of each day – and how we spend them – that makes up our lives.

We can either evaluate everything based on God's word and will, or we can waste them on things of this world.

That doesn't necessarily mean that God wants us to give up everything fun. And especially not every ministry. He simply wants us to surrender and commit everything in our lives to Him.

The question is whether we will listen.

We've already had a prayer time today, but I'd like to have another. Living intimately with God is the only way to live a stress-free life and prayer is essential to that intimate walk.

Look up and use the lines on the following page to write out Luke 7:46-49.

_____
_____
_____
_____
_____
_____
_____
_____
_____
_____
_____
_____
_____

Use this scripture as the basis for your prayer time with God as we close out today. Seek what He is saying to you, what He is trying to teach you, and ask for the strength and wisdom to follow His leading.

~~~*~~~
"Be still, and know that I am God! I will be
honored by every nation. I will be
honored throughout the world."
Psalm 46:10
~~~*~~~

Section 3

As I review section 2 and get ready to move on, I realize that I didn't even really touch on being overwhelmed by the things we have to do. We talked about praying over our calendars, surrendering them to the Lord, and being willing (and even taking the initial steps towards) changing them, but we didn't talk about the overwhelmedness. The stress of it all.

Therefore, we're going to pause there a bit today. We're going to focus on the words "have to." These words seem to come with a sense of obligation and burden.

When we "have to" do something, there is no joy in it. No service in love. No outpouring. And it's the opposite of how God desires us to serve.

Instead of looking at the things in life as a "have to," what would happen if our perspective became "get to?"

It would radically change our lives.

We would recognize everything – yes, EVERYTHING – we get to do as a privilege. Which it all is, by the grace of God and especially if we are walking in obedience to Him.

Think of the single mothers living in poverty around the world, and possibly around the corner. What choices do you have for your children that she never will?

Think of the person born with a physical disability that prevents easy, fluid body movement. What are you able to do that they never will?

Think of the people who work their fingers to the bone day in and day out, not to earn enough money for the pleasures of life, but just to have enough food to survive until the next day.

Think of the person who relies on public transportation, cares for an incapacitated or severely ill family member, deals with pain every day, has no family or church support, has never heard the name of Jesus? What can you do that they don't even know are options?

You may even fit into one of these categories. The truth is that we all have the ability to do things that someone else in the world doesn't. We can count it as a "have to" and be weighed down by it, or we can count it as a "get to" and serve from an overflowing of love.

This is very scriptural – that we serve out of and are fueled by God's love for us.

> If I could speak all the languages of earth
> and of angels, but didn't love others, I
> would only be a noisy gong or a clanging
> cymbal. If I had the gift of prophecy, and
> if I understood all of God's secret plans
> and possessed all knowledge, and if I had
> such faith that I could move mountains,
> but didn't love others, I would be nothing.
> If I gave everything I have to the poor
> and even sacrificed my body, I could
> boast about it; but if I didn't love
> others, I would have gained nothing.
> 1 Corinthians 13:1-3

Most of us are familiar with 1 Corinthians 13 as being the love chapter and describing what love looks like. I wonder, though, how often we examine this part of the chapter in reference to how we're serving the Lord.

Take a moment to reread the verses in light of how you approach activities, responsibilities, and commitments.

Use the space below to record what God shows you:

_____

_____

_____

_____

_____

I wish we could sit down and talk about what He's teaching you! I'm sure it'd be a blessing and a great benefit. Hopefully to you, but definitely to me.

Did you notice how nothing we do matters if it isn't in and out of love? That includes all the things that fill our calendars.

We've talked about changing or giving up some of those things, but the truth of the matter is sometimes we only have so much ability to lighten our schedules. When we aren't able to do so (because God's leading us to stay right where we are) we can instead change our perspective.

We have the power to go from "have to" to "get to."

We can fix our eyes on Jesus and the eternal and do

everything with thanksgiving "as a representative of the Lord Jesus." {Colossians 3:17}

We'll close out here. As we do and head into today's prayer time, let's pray for God to fill us and draw us so very close to Him that we will not only let go of the things He hasn't called us to do, but do the things He has called us to do out of love and joy. Ask God to remind you of His strength and provision through "the message about Christ, in all its richness." {Colossians 3:16a}

~~~*~~~
Devote yourselves to prayer with an
alert mind and a thankful heart.
Colossians 4:2
~~~*~~~

Section 4

I know that not everyone gets stressed over schedules and overwhelmed with too much on their calendars. It's still good to evaluate the things we do, how we spend our time, and the choices we make based on scripture. To lay everything at the feet of Jesus and seek His will – in everything.

I hope even if busyness and over-commitment aren't stress factors for you, you've stuck with us. We have talked about so much, but have many more areas of stress to address.

Today, we're going to focus on the second part of the verses in Mark 4 we've been discussing. It's the second part of our discussion began yesterday:

> They are "overwhelmed with worries about...the things they want to get."

We today, I believe, more than ever before live in a culture that invites envy, jealousy, and comparison. We see what others have on TV, in movies, on social media, and as we drive by multitudes of houses. We know what we don't have and what so many others do.

I've heard from many people that they grew up dirt poor, but never knew it. They were isolated from other people who had more than them, so they never knew what they didn't have. They were happy and content because they had family and love.

Long gone are those days for almost everyone living in America.

You may be wondering what all this has to do with stress, or stress-free living. First, the scripture we're working through reveals that the things we want to get can distract us from our devotion to God. Let's look at it one more time:

> The seed that fell among the thorns represents others who hear God's word, **but all too quickly the message is crowded out** by the worries of this life, the lure of wealth, and **the desire for other things, so no fruit is produced.**
> Mark 4:18-19 {emphasis added}

This overwhelmed or crowding out is clearly not an obedient, God-centered life. It is contradictory to the life Jesus called us to.

Let's take a few moments to read John 15:1-17. It's a long section, so I won't have you write it, but there's no real way to get the whole picture of how important–essential, really–producing fruit in Jesus' name is.

Read through this amazing passage and use the lines below to record parts that stand out or anything God's revealing to you:

_____

_____

_____

_____

_____

_____

Did you notice that producing fruit is mentioned seven times in this one passage? The one that really stands out to me, and when paired with the verses out of Mark 4 we're studying can be very eye-opening and scary, is this:

> When you produce much fruit, you
> are my true disciples. This brings
> great glory to my Father.
> John 15:8

True disciples produce much fruit. We do not bear fruit when we are distracted by the worries of this life and desire for things.

God desires our hearts and our whole lives. When we spend a majority of our time, energy, and effort in obtaining things, we are missing out on God's best for us, bringing glory to His name, and great joy.

> I have told you these things so
> that you will be filled with my joy.
> Yes, your joy will overflow!
> John 15:11

There are also many other places in scripture which clearly direct us to seek God and not stuff:

> Don't store up treasures here on earth,
> where moths eat them and rust destroys
> them, and where thieves break in and steal.
> Store you treasures in heaven, where
> moths and rust cannot destroy, and
> thieves do not break in and steal.
> Matthew 6:19-20

> Then he said, "Beware! Guard against
> every kind of greed. Life is not
> measured by how much you own."
> Luke 12:15

> For the world offers only craving for
> physical pleasure, a craving for everything
> we see, and pride in our achievements
> and possessions. They are not from
> the Father, but are from this world.
> 1 John 2:16

God is clear. When we desire things, we rob ourselves of joy and Him of due glory and honor.

Isn't that why we do much of what we do? To receive:
- A newer, shinier, faster, bigger possession
- Accolades, applause, and acknowledgement
- Experiences that are fun and make memories
- Comfort and contentment
- Fill in the blank _____

I feel like so much of life has been consumed by the desire of the temporal – and stress in working towards getting it!

We spent a few days lifting up in prayer and laying down at Jesus' feet the items of our calendars. Now it's time to examine the desires of our hearts. What are we striving to accomplish or get that is choking our relationship with Jesus?

As we close today, let us bear our souls before the Creator and Sustainer of all things. In prayer, seek God, ask Him to reveal the desires that have snuck into your heart. Open yourself for Him to reveal how things near and dear to your heart are distracting you from His Word, worship, and working on Kingdom things. Then ask Him to do a mighty work in you so that you will be able to abide in Him and produce much spiritual fruit.

~~~*~~~
Wherever your treasure is, there the desires of your heart will also be.
Matthew 6:21
~~~*~~~

Day 5

Did you find yesterday to be hard? I did! There is not much like cracking open our hearts for God to examine them. Therefore, before we move on to closing out this week, I'd love to give you some time to reflect on what God's saying to you.

Checking in:
What from yesterday was the hardest? _____
_____
_____
_____
_____

What from yesterday brought fresh revelation to you?
_____
_____
_____
_____

What is one step that will take you from where you are (in talking about desires of your heart) to where God is leading you to go? _____
_____
_____
_____

It may seem like working to change our hearts and desires may add more stress to life, but even if it does, it is part of that short term sacrifice for long term rewards we've talked about. God has so much more in store for us than we generally can even imagine, but the path there is also often very different from the life we've pictured for ourselves.

As a reminder of why it's worth it to examine our schedules, our desires, our lives, write out John 15:11 below.

_____

_____

_____

_____

I hope that's encouraging to you! God desires to fill us with joy until we overflow with it!! He is truly amazing in His grace, mercy, and love like that.

I feel like we need to pause here and praise Him. Will you join me?

Father, thank You for Your unrelenting grace. For Your unmatched love. For Your mercy that is new EVERY DAY. You are great and alone worthy of praise. I lift up Your name on high and will proclaim Your greatness and wondrous deeds until the day You call me home. Hallelujah! Praise You, Jesus! I love You!

Now, write your own praise/prayer to the Lord.

_____

_____

_____

_____

_____

_____

_____

_____

I hope you are uplifted and encouraged by our mini praise session. I anticipate that the words the Lord gave you to add your own praise were powerful and brought great joy to you.

Oh, how I would love to just sit here a while and give glory and honor to the only One worthy. Worship and praise are truly the best antidotes to the poison of stress.

It is a scary thing to turn over our hearts and desires, our schedules and our calendars, our activities, accolades, and accomplishments to the Lord. We've been taught to hold them tight, and truly, they often become idols.

We have a part in the work of God, but not out of our own longings, efforts, and strengths. It's in the laying down of everything in our lives, our very lives themselves, and letting God have it all that we find both the direction of and strength to do God's will.

It's in this letting go that we eliminate stress and find incomprehensible peace.

> Now may the God of peace—who
> brought up from the dead our Lord Jesus,
> the great Shepherd of the sheep, and
> ratified an eternal covenant with his blood—
> may he equip you with all you need for
> doing his will. May he produce in you,
> through the power of Jesus Christ, every
> good thing that is pleasing to him. All
> glory to him forever and ever! Amen.
> Hebrews 13:20-21

Have you ever had this thought?: "If God can raise Jesus from the dead – from the dead! From physical death, gone, all hope is lost, rotting flesh in a grave death– to life, that truly NOTHING is impossible for Him! Especially keeping me in perfect peace, because, after all, He is the God of peace!"

I wish I had thoughts like this more often. It certainly helps me refocus off myself, my desires, my schedule, and my stress.

We have to live on this earth. With calendars, schedules, activities, obligations, material things, and a flesh that tends to stray from its Maker. While it often seems impossible to not be bogged down by all this, it is possible. The key is to "fix our eyes on Jesus."

Easily said. More difficultly done, but possible.

Most of us are familiar with this phrase from Hebrews 12:2. In working on this section and deciding which translation to use (the New Living Translation, which I mostly use, didn't word it in this familiar way, so I was looking for one that did), I felt led to go to the Amplified Bible. It is most interesting how this verse is translated. It confirms that this verse is the exact one we need to help counter all the stress and distractions we've been covering this week.

> Looking away [from all that will distract]
> to Jesus, Who is the Leader *and* the Source
> of our faith [giving the first incentive for our
> belief] and is also is Finisher [bringing it to
> maturity and perfection].
> Hebrews 12:2a (AMP)

An essential step is purposefully and intentionally looking away from all the things that distract us to Jesus. As we lay down and submit every detail of our lives seeking to live in obedience and gratitude, He will provide everything we need.

- The next step on the path
- What to give up
- What to continue doing
- What new things He wants to bring to our lives
- Everything we need for this life
- Comfort
- Joy
- Peace

And so much more!

As we close today and this week, this is where we will hold our prayers. Join me in seeking the Lord's will and strength to follow it. To throw off all these things of the world that hinder us, choke us, stress us, and crowd out the Word and will of God. To fix our eyes on Him and have our hearts desires conformed to His. To live a life not focused on the temporal, but on the eternal and the

Lord who provides.

~~~*~~~

Don't copy the behavior and customs of
this world, but let God transform you into a
new person by changing the way you think.
Then you will learn to know God's will for you,
which is good and pleasing and perfect.
Romans 12:2

~~~*~~~

Week 2 Group Discussion Questions

(1) What was it like examining your calendar, commitments, and responsibilities?

(2) Did God reveal any specific things that He wants you to change or give up? What steps have you or are you going to take to make those changes?

(3) How has this study changed your view on the worries, obligations, and desires for things and how these affect our relationship with God?

(4) Discuss this statement: "It's hard to face, but we often opt for stress in our lives instead of the King of Peace."

(5) How does it change things to look at everything we do as an opportunity to do it out of love and not obligation?

(6) Have you ever thought about stress and worry being like weeds that strangle the Word of God and choke out our opportunities to bear fruit? Discuss.

(7) How does knowing/being reminded that nothing is impossible for God and He is trustworthy with every detail of your life impact how you live each day and handle stress?

Week 3
Relationships

Section 1

God created us as relational creatures. He desires an intimate, close relationship with Him. He has also given us people in our lives to have relationships with. The original plan was for us to encourage, equip, and edify each other. What else is a helpmate to do?

> Then the Lord God said, "It is not good
> for man to be alone. I will make a
> helper who is just right for him."
> Genesis 2:18

At first, everything was perfect. Sometime after, sin entered the picture, and with it strife and strain in human relationships. (See Genesis 3.)

God's plan is still for us to be in relationship with each other, even to the point of perfect unity.

> Make every effort to keep yourselves
> united in the Spirit, binding yourselves
> together with peace.
> Ephesians 4:3

The fact that Paul starts this statement (and countless other scriptures about relationships in and out of the body of Christ) with the words "make every effort" should clue us in right from the beginning that relationships are hard. They take almost constant effort.

Just in case you didn't know that already.

I think, personally, that relationships have always been challenging. All it takes is a quick glance through Biblical stories and ancient anthologies to realize that people haven't gotten along well and easily since Adam and Eve were thrown out of the garden. For goodness sake, the first set of siblings experienced envy and murder.

You can't get any more contentious than that.

Things have improved and worsened overall in different time periods. There have been horrendous things done to people as a whole during certain eras, and in others people have encouraged respect and care for each other. Individually, however, relationships have always tended to be more work than most people want to put into them.

I think this is especially true in the self-focused, just do it culture, where fun and pleasure are the ultimate goals, and "if it feels good" is the ultimate measure for decision-making.

While Christians tout love and the word says their aim is to put love at a high standard, an examination of the state our world and relationships are in big trouble. Love is clearly not the ultimate goal of most people.

Well, biblical, God-driven, sacrificial love isn't.

Thus we have stress in relationships.

God has been doing some interesting things in my life over the last six months to reveal the stress that relationships can cause in life. I won't go into details, because they don't matter. However, I want to acknowledge the different situations that can cause stress in our lives. To not brush over any possible type of situation that you may be going through. To show how God can reveal Himself and bring His healing to any and every relationship.

The list below is not exhaustive, and praise the Lord isn't all personal to me. Some of them can be considered situational or due to circumstances, but we will focus on the relational aspect.

Marriage – any time two people try to live and walk through life together there will be conflict and stress. Even under "normal" circumstances. That doesn't even touch adultery, debt, deceit, different life goals, differences in child-rearing, abuse (verbal, emotional, and/or physical), or a host of other special situations.

Parenting – children come with their own challenges. Personality conflicts and children at ages we find hard to deal with cause stress. (Let's get real about this! It doesn't mean we don't love our children with everything we have, but our love doesn't make it all easy, roses and butterflies, either.) Again, this is under "normal" circumstances. Then we could talk about children with challenges such as autism, cancer, emotional health issues, physical disabilities, learning disabilities, or being survivors of some kind of abuse.

Other family relationships – parents, siblings, in-laws, etc. The more people we add in, the more personalities, personal desires and perspectives are brought in. Different family backgrounds can cause conflict, as well as past history that comes with hurts and hard feelings. And we could always add some of the special circumstances from the above two sections.

Friendships – while friendships are often a blessing, they can also come with conflict. There can also be friendships that are out of balance or toxic.

(On that note, any relationship we have can be toxic – with our spouse, child, parent, sibling, etc. The closer the toxic relationship is to us, the more it affects us.)

Coworkers – work environments are sometimes a place of joy, friendships, and mutual encouragement and growth. Sometimes they are places of conflict, competition, and cautiousness.

Church members – while this should be the last place that should be a source of stressful relationships, the truth is that brothers and sisters in Christ are still human. There is always potential for hurt feelings, conflicting opinions, and personality clashes. This is why Paul wrote commands like the one found in Ephesians 4:3.

Let's write that verse out below, as it's a great start for this week and covers ALL the relationships listed above (and those few remaining that aren't listed):

_____
_____
_____
_____
_____

I love that this verse talks about peace. We've looked intimately already about the fact that peace is the opposite of stress.

Wouldn't you like to have peace in all of your relationships? I know I would!

The thing we tend to do, however, is try to change people, convince people, or pray them into a different person. Or to see our perspective. To come around to our way of thinking.

This is our default. However, this strategy will never work. Because it's based in manipulation, selfishness, and our desire to be in control and have things our way.

The strategy for handling stressful relationships by trying to cajole, change, or correct another person's behavior is not only not biblical, it actually causes more damage.

It hinders our walk with God because we think we have the power to make things different. We aren't willing to trust God with that person, that relationship, for Him to do His work.

This is a hard thing to face: Our desire to change other people is a lack of faith in the Lord, Creator, and Sustainer of the universe.

While it is the Lord's responsibility and ability to change people and relationships, we are not let completely off the hook. Ephesians 4:3 tells us this. So does Romans 12:18:

> Do all that you can to live in
> peace with everyone.

Underline those first five words. We have a responsibility.

So what is "all that {we} can"?

The first thing is to go back to what we did with our schedules and calendars. We offer every single person and relationship in our lives to the Lord.

We'll start again with simply praying. Submitting these people and relationships to the Father who loves us with an everlasting, faithful, perfect love. The One who knows best how to lead us in our dealings and communications with those in our lives.

Take time with the Lord. Take each name to Him one by one. This will take more time than you feel you can give, but truly, how can we afford not to take our relationships to Him? He knows, loves, and desires to work in their lives much more than we do.

That same everlasting, faithful, perfect love He has for us, He also has for every single person in our lives.

I don't know what relationship challenges you may have or are facing right now. But the Lord does. We will get to more work and actions we can take as we move forward, but let us agree with the Holy Spirit in what He wants to do in us and through us in our relationships first.

I pray that your time with the Lord will be sweet, even if hard, and that He will start even on this first day of looking at living stress-free in our relationships to reveal His unmatched, incomprehensible peace to you.

~~~*~~~
I urge you, first of all, to pray for all people.
Ask God to help them; intercede on their
behalf, and give thanks for them.
1 Timothy 2:1
~~~*~~~

Section 2

I'm starting to feel like a broken record. I so wish we could sit down and talk about what God is revealing to you, doing in you. I can only imagine what work is going on through your prayer times and intentionality in looking at relationships.

I wonder how often we really examine our relationships, especially as possible sources of stress.

I guess we kind of know that relationships stress us out sometimes, but do we really look at them from the lens of learning to live stress-free.

Remember, there's a difference between stressors in our lives and stress. We can't always eliminate the stressors – that would mean giving up all our relationships! So, unless we're ready to give it all up and go live like recluses, we'd be better off to figure out how to manage and maintain better relationships.

Besides, God created us as relational beings.

Remember back in the garden of Eden? God said it wasn't good for man to be alone. He wasn't just talking about Adam, He was talking about us all.

Throughout scripture, there are dozens of references to "each other." Some references are to strife. Some to simply living life together. Others, many found in the New Testament, are about us loving each other and living, as Ephesians 4:3 states, in unity with each other.

Let's look at a handful of them:

...so it is with Christ's body. We are many parts of one body, and we all belong to each other.
Romans 12:5

Love each other with genuine affection, and take delight in honoring each other.
Romans 12:10

So then, let us aim for harmony in the church and try to build each other up.
Romans 14:19

This makes for harmony among the members, so that all the members care for each other.
1 Corinthians 12:25

Dear brothers and sisters, I close my letter with these last words: Be joyful. Grow in maturity. Encourage each other. Live in harmony and peace. Then the God of love and peace will be with you.
2 Corinthians 13;11

So encourage each other and build each other up, just as you are already doing.
1 Thessalonians 5:11

Keep on loving each other as brothers and sisters.
Hebrews 13:1

You were cleansed from your sins when you obeyed the truth, so now you must show sincere love to each other as brothers and sisters. Love each other deeply with all your heart.
1 Peter 1:22

Did you notice any themes? Did anything stand out to you? What is God saying specifically to you through these verses?

_____

_____

_____

_____

_____

I hope you can hear Him talking! I most certainly can.

Before we look at these verses a bit closer, let me say, confess, really, how convicting these verses are to me. I so wish that I could report to you that I would score an A+ on this relationship test. The truth of the matter is, however, that I have much growth yet to happen.

The verses above specifically talk about relationships with brothers and sisters in Christ – which could be fellow church members (either the church we attend or the many other ones out there), our spouse, children, parents, siblings, coworkers, friends, etc.

Or it could not. Many of us have many non-believers in our lives. This does not excuse us from loving behavior, though.

> Therefore, whenever we have the opportunity, we should do good to everyone – especially to those in the family of faith.
> Galatians 6:10

Let me highlight a couple of phrases for us:

- **whenever we have the opportunity**

- **do good to everyone.**

We have opportunities every day. I wonder how many we miss.

Have you noticed that this section is about what we can do to help our relationships be more peaceful?

How do you feel about this responsibility? _____
_____
_____
_____
_____

As I said before, I'm not sure how often we take a glance at how we treat our relationships.

If we were to, however, I bet we'd find great room for improvement. I sure know I do!

*****

Brief Caveat:
I felt led to include this tidbit of advice in this section. It can be transformational and life-changing.

Much of what we stress over in our relationships are little things that don't really matter that much. A lot of times it's because we want things done our way. One thing

I've learned is that there is bondage in trying to control what others do, how they do it, and when they do it.

On the flipside, there is freedom in letting others do things their way and in their timing. It may mean we have to get uncomfortable and hold our tongues a bit more – okay, maybe bite them to the point of risking cutting all the way through – but it will greatly reduce our stress.

Before you think I don't know what I'm talking about let me share a couple of stories.

Many years ago, but after my husband and I had been dating several years, I was at his house fixing food for us to go out on the boat for the day. He said he'd be back in a few minutes. Five minutes passed. Then thirty. Then an hour. I began to fume. Until I realized I was the only one affected by my anger.

I knew him well enough to know that he had almost no ability to keep track of time and had most likely just gotten into a good conversation with the neighbors (which he had) and figured I was busy getting things done (which I was). I decided then and there to try not to put my expectations on him.

I've had many, many opportunities to put this into practice, not only with timing, but with how things are done, or with him not making things a priority that I think should be a priority. Me trying to control him (or anyone else I'm in a relationship with) stresses me the most, but also puts strain on the relationship.

So, I couldn't ignore the important aspect of loving better by letting go of the things we try to control and not placing our expectations on what things need to be priority, how things are done, and when they're done. (On minor things. When things are major and are really important, that's when it's time to stand your ground, albeit in a loving way. A good question to ask is, "How important is this really?")

*****

Flip back a few pages and reread the verses listed. The responsibility for harmony and peace in relationships is laid on each of us. We can't make other people fulfill their part of a relationship, but we can certainly do our part.

Our part is to:

- Acknowledge we belong to each other (contrary to the modern/secular concept of we only belong to and are accountable to ourselves)
- Love each other genuinely
- Honor each other – and delight in doing so!
- Build each other up
- Care for each other
- Encourage each other
- Love each other *as brothers and sisters*
- Love each other sincerely
- Love each other deeply

I hope this list doesn't stress you out. It is very weighty – if we look at what we can do in and of ourselves. But if we search the scriptures on what we're supposed to do and seek God's will and strength to do it, it is possible.

It is from God and His love that we are able to pour ourselves selflessly and sacrificially into others.

> This is real love – not that we loved God, but that he loved us and sent his Son as a sacrifice to take away our sins. Dear friends, since God loved us that much, we surely ought to love each other. No one has ever seen God. But if we love each other, God lives in us, and his love is brought to full expression in us.
> 1 John 4:11-12

It is in the diving into God's Word, soaking in and filling up on His love, and laying down our relationships at His feet that we do the greatest work. These are the essential steps to be able to love, honor, build up, care for and encourage those we're in relationship with. Not by trying harder, but by trusting the Lord more.

That's how we will close and pray. Join me in once again praying for those we're in closest relationship with. Those we may have the most conflictual relationship with. Ask the Lord to remind you of His great, faithful, generous, never-ending, love. Ask Him to show you in His word the depth and breadth of His love. Ask Him to fill you up so much with His love that you can't help but overflow it to those around you. Then thank and praise Him for that love and for the work He is already doing in your relationships that you can't even see yet.

~~~*~~~
> May God, who gives this patience and encouragement, help you live in complete harmony with each other, as is fitting for followers of Christ Jesus.
> Romans 15:5

~~~*~~~

Section 3

I hope your time with God this week has been fruitful. I hope that He is illuminating your relationships and showing you how they can be more of a joy-bringer than a stressor.

That doesn't mean they will become perfect. Any time interaction between two humans is involved, there will be some level of conflict, stress and difficulties. However, we are moving forward in how we can live obedient to the Lord and His call to love and how that obedience (and soaking in of His great love for us) can positively affect our relationships.

Now on to something even more difficult than loving someone deeply, sincerely, and genuinely.

Forgiveness

It's interesting. When I started writing this Bible study I never would've guessed we'd have ended up here. I honestly didn't know we'd be talking about relationships at all, but as the Lord leads, there I go (most of the time).

The truth of the matter is, when we really open ourselves to the sources of stress in our lives, relationships probably make up a big portion.

And quite often, a major contributor to stress in relationships is un-forgiveness.

Studies, experience, and scripture all agree that holding on to hurts is detrimental to our health – emotionally, physically, mentally, and spiritually. Yet we often refuse to let go of offenses.

Part of the reason for this is a misunderstanding of what forgiveness really is and really means.

Another reason we don't want to let go is because we live in a culture that holds revenge up as a worthy and attainable goal.

Still another reason is sometimes we are more comfortable being the victim (even though we would almost never admit this – even to ourselves).

In relationships there always has to be forgiveness. Because we're all imperfect and will hurt those we love no matter what.

Now, there are certainly different levels of hurt. There's the said something in anger hurt. There's the made a negative choice hurt. There's complete betrayal of trust hurt. There's years of disrespect, contradiction, and even abuse hurt.

Here me clearly on this, though: The level of hurt – whether it's a one or a ten – does not determine your ability or need to forgive. Pain is pain and will damage you from the inside out if you don't purge it.

What are some relationships you've had in the past where you've forgiven and experienced healing?

_____

_____

_____

_____

What are some relationships you've had in the past where you're still hurting?

_____

_____

_____

Now consider your current relationships. Some of them may be with the people you thought of above. Some of them may be newer relationships with less history. Are there any recent hurts that you have?

Is there forgiveness that needs to happen for you to move on and heal from?

Because our minds, bodies and spirits are intertwined and impossible to separate, holding on to offenses always causes stress. Whether we acknowledge it or not. This is why God commanded us over and over to forgive. Not for the other person, although restoration often takes place in forgiveness and both parties are blessed, but mostly for us.

Forgiveness helps bring healing and health to our minds, bodies, and spirits.

Un-forgiveness, on the other hand, puts up barriers in our fellowship with God.

> But when you are praying, first forgive
> anyone you are holding a grudge
> against, so that your Father in
> heaven will forgive your sins, too.
> Mark 11:25

Let's discuss one of the reasons we often refuse or resist forgiveness: a misunderstanding of what forgiveness is.

Many believe that forgiveness sends the message that the behavior wasn't that bad or didn't really hurt.

This couldn't be further from the truth. Forgiveness says, "What you did was wrong, it hurt me greatly, but I won't let it hurt me anymore."

There's the thought that forgiveness lets the offender off the hook in the sense of consequences.

In some cases, this is true. But there are many scriptural examples of God forgiving someone yet not removing their consequences. David comes to mind, in reference to his adultery with Bathsheba.

Another misconception is that forgiveness means complete relationship restoration. This can be true. There are people who've gone through great hurts, experienced forgiveness and a relationship that was not just restored to what it was before, but sometimes and even closer, healthier relationship.

This is not always the case, however. Nor should it be. God does not want us to be in toxic relationships where offenses continue. (Usually. There are times He calls us to remain in relationships where the person doesn't repent, or repeatedly offends. It's a matter of deep prayer and truly seeking the Lord's will. For further study on this, see the book of Hosea.)

While forgiveness can mean full restoration in a relationship, it can also mean partial restoration. Where the relationship changes to protect us from greater hurt, but we don't completely cut that person out of our lives.

There are also cases where a relationship does need to be completely eliminated. This doesn't mean that forgiveness hasn't happened. It just means that despite forgiveness the relationship should not continue.

Given these truths about forgiveness, I hope you can see why God commands us over and over to forgive. It is for our good and His glory.

There is so much more we could say about forgiveness, but we are running out of time.

(I recommend considering any or all of the following books if you need to dig into this topic further: *Free of Charge* by Miroslav Volf; *Forgiveness* by Kay Arthur; *The Gift of Forgiveness* by Charles Stanley.)

As we move to close out today, we're going to review several scriptures on forgiveness. We'll also use these verses as the foundation for our closing prayer today.

Remember, offenses and wounds cause stress in our lives. They affect us emotionally, mentally, physically, and spiritually.

Forgiveness is not easy, but it's essential to living a stress-free, abundant life. You will probably not work through everything today. Or this week. Maybe not even this month. But hopefully reading, meditating on, and praying these scriptures will be a big step on the journey.

~~~*~~~

Always be humble and gentle. Be patient with each other, making allowance for each other's faults because of your love.
Ephesians 4;2

Get rid of all bitterness, rage, anger, harsh words, and slander, as well as all types of evil behavior. Instead, be kind to each other, tenderhearted, forgiving one another, just as God through Christ has forgiven you.
Ephesians 4:31-32

Make allowance for each other's faults, and forgive anyone who offends you. Remember, the Lord forgave you, so you must forgive others.
Colossians 3:13

Most important of all, continue to show deep love for each other, for love covers a multitude of sins.
1 Peter 4:8
~~~*~~~

Section 4

I almost feel like we need to spend today reviewing day three. Forgiveness is such a huge topic that one day doesn't seem adequate. I'll trust, however, if you need to dive into the topic on your own, outside this brief study, you'll prayerfully do so.

So far, we've talked about how we can love others better and forgive others offenses to help reduce stress in relationships. In other words, the things that are within our control and realm of change. Now we're going to address the things that are out of our control – other people.

Being from a family which is speckled with people who've struggled with addiction, one of my favorite prayers is the Serenity Prayer. We're going to look at it as we start today's study.

> God, grant me the serenity
> to accept the things I can't change,
> the courage to change the things I can,
> and the wisdom to know the difference.

There is great wisdom in knowing that you can change your own thoughts and behaviors, allow God to mold you and shape your beliefs, ideals, and ideas to match His, but you can never, ever, under any circumstance do this for another human being.

Ever.

Therefore, we can love more and better, we can forgive and let go, but we will not ever change another person.

Now, it is near impossible for one person in a relationship to change without the other person(s) in that relationship being affected. They may change some things just because if you're not talking, behaving, and reacting like you always have, it will change the nature of your interactions with that person. Almost always.

There will be much about the people in our lives that will not change, though, no matter how much we change. There will still be conflict. There will still be differences of opinion. There will still be hurts and offenses. There will still be some stress associated with the people we love.

This is the nature of humans living in a fallen world. As long as we are bound by our flesh, all of these things will be a part of life.

So what do we do with them?

We accept what we can't change.

We pray over our relationships.

We sometimes walk away from relationships.

I don't say this lightly. Relationships are difficult and challenging and most of the time they are worth fighting for. When we work through issues, forgive, love, and put God first in our relationships they can blossom and grow into something amazingly beautiful.

But there are times when the relationship is so toxic it can't be salvaged.

This should only be done after praying faithfully, listening to God's guidance, and making every effort towards the health of the relationship.

We're talking about relationships in general here, but I must point out that there's a huge difference between walking away from a friendship, an acquaintance and walking away from a close family member or spouse. No matter what the situation, we should always consult scripture and the Lord through prayer. Godly counsel is a helpful tool, also.

Checking in:
Think about the relationships in your life that are a source of stress. Pray over them again. Ask God to show you how you can apply the lessons learned already in this study (the things you can change). Then ask Him to help you accept the things you can't. To love each one of these people, faults and all, in a supernatural way.

What has God revealed to you in your time of prayer?
_____
_____
_____
_____
_____

So now we're going to talk about those things we can't change. Because they are going to be present.

First, I'd like to share a little bit of my story that God in His sovereignty has let me live out the last few months leading up to this study.

I shared earlier that my family moved in with my in-laws. It really is a good situation, we are very blessed to have this home to live in while we work towards building our own home. However, any time you put two families in the same household there will be challenges.

Challenges around different ways of doing things. Challenges of having different perspectives. Challenges around sharing a kitchen and living space. Challenges around having four active kids around older adults on a daily basis. Challenges of living a little bit differently.

There is nothing I can do to change my situation right now. There's nothing I can do to change some of the differences in ways of doing things or seeing things. I can do the best I can do to be loving, kind, thoughtful, and gracious. But that will not resolve or remove every challenge.

What I can do, however, is change my perspective on my situation and my relationships. So, even though I have no control over so much, I do have control over my attitude and perspective.

This is true in all of our relationships. We can approach other's flaws and differences from a worldly perspective and grumble or complain. Or we can approach them from an eternal perspective.

We can focus on the differences and challenges, or we can focus on the similarities and what we're in agreement on.

Let's look at two verses to remind ourselves which is the approach the Lord desires us to take.

Look up and write out Philippians 2:14:

_____

_____

_____

Now look up and write out Philippians 4:8:

_____

_____

_____

_____

_____

_____

When we choose arguing, complaining, and a critical spirit we are heaping stress both on ourselves and the other person. Wanting everything our way and trying to change other people will always multiply our stress.

On the other hand, when we choose to focus on what is truthful, lovely, encouraging, and good, we foster peace.

Choosing a right attitude and perspective is on us. It may feel like it lets the other person off the hook, but they're not ours to hook, reel in, skin, and fry up. It's the Lord's job to call, convict, and carry people through change.

It's our job to live with them doing everything within our power to live at peace with them.

Even their faults that sometimes stress us out.

One more caveat before we close. Sometimes we do have the authority to effect change in those around us. Especially with children.

We're not talking about bad behaviors that we have to put up with while maintaining a right attitude. Sometimes the things our children do (even grown up children) simply aren't acceptable. In those cases we have the right, and really the obligation, to put limits around sinful/harmful behavior and hold them accountable to their choices. We do not have to accept sin in our homes.

There are also situations where a spouse or grown child, other family member or friend has major issues such as drug addiction, alcoholism, porn addiction, promiscuity, vulgarity, etc.

It is not our job to "fix" them, but neither do we have to accept these behaviors. If you are facing such a situation – which is extremely high on the stress level chart – I highly recommend you seek godly counsel and educate yourself about creating healthy boundaries.

We'll close today by praying through Philippians 2:14 and 4:18. Ask the Lord to strengthen you to do EVERYTHING without arguing, complaining, grumbling, faultfinding, or questioning. Ask Him to work in you to keep an eternal focus and let your thoughts and your words be full of grace, honorable, true, pure, lovely, admirable and excellent. And don't forget to ask our Heavenly Father for patience for ourselves as we are molded to be more like Him and for others around us as they too are being molded – even if we can't see it.

~~~*~~~
Always be humble and gentle. Be
patient with each other, making
allowance for each other's faults
because of your love.
Ephesians 4:2
~~~*~~~

Section 5

As we close out this week on relationships, let's turn to the one relationship that's most important – our relationship with the Lord.

The truth is, we are all fallible and tend to want to do things our way, but the Lord and His ways are perfect.

> "God's way is perfect. All the Lord's
> promises prove true. He is a shield for
> all who look to him for protection."
> 2 Samuel 22:31 ~ Psalm 18:30

When we're willing to trust Him with our relationships, to do the work in the lives of the people we love, we are only giving Him what is rightly His.

Just last week I lost a dear Christian friend and mentor. He died suddenly and unexpectedly of a massive stroke at age 57. It was devastating. To his wife. His children. His grandchildren. His parents. His siblings. To everyone who knew him. He was a great man of faith and doing amazing things for the spread of the gospel. None of us could fully grasp God's taking him home when He did.

Even from the next day, however, we began to see God working through this dear brother's death in unique ways. The memorial/celebration of life service for him was beautiful. One thing during the service stood out above the rest. That's when his mother got up and spoke.

She used the opportunity, in her unimaginable grief, to remind us all that our children are on loan. They are not ours. They do not belong to us, but they belong to God and we are simply entrusted with guiding them through life.

As I reflected on her words and the truth of them, I was also reminded of some verses we recently went through in church.

Read through Genesis 22:1-14.

Most of us are familiar with this story, but I think we (like with most familiar Bible stories) breeze past it too quickly.

You may be scratching your head in wonder at why I'd pick this particular passage in a Bible study on reducing, dealing with, and managing stress.

Or maybe you can see where this is going. In order to have peace in our relationships, it's supremely helpful to recognize that no one in our lives really belong to us, but to the Lord.

When we examine Abraham's willingness to personally sacrifice his son – his most prized relationship – for the Lord, it is unfathomable to us. We don't have a clue how one could ever do this.

The same is often true for an emotional laying down of our loved ones. We don't want to hand them over to the Lord.

Something I was shown through the sermons around this verse was the journey and many, many opportunities Abraham had to learn to trust the Lord and walk in obedience to Him.

It was a long, difficult road Abraham took to get to this point. But He had learned that the Lord was trustworthy, completely faithful to His promises, and holy. Therefore, he was willing to trust the Lord with the very life of his son.

Record verse 8 from this passage here:

_____

_____

_____

_____

Abraham did not know how God would provide, he just believed He would.

Abraham couldn't see God's provision, but he trusted it was there.

We often don't know how God will provide or move in the life of a loved one, *but we can believe that He will*.

We often can't see how God is providing or moving in the heart of a loved one, *but we can trust that He is*.

When we choose to believe and trust the Lord with the people we love, we eliminate our stress and worry over them. We no longer have to carry the burden of what they will do, what will happen to them, or how their life will turn out.

This doesn't mean God won't call us to some action. Abraham still had to parent Isaac and teach him to know and love the Lord. It just means our actions are motivated out of love and trust, instead of fear and anxiety.

Who do you need to lay at Jesus' feet today?

Use the rest of your study time today to pray over this person(s), their situation, and your relationship with them. Offer them up to the Lord and commit to seek His guidance and grace to relinquish them to Him. He, after all, loves them more than we ever could.

~~~*~~~
Trust in *and* rely confidently on the LORD
with all your heart And do not rely on
your own insight *or* understanding.
Proverbs 3:5 {AMP}
~~~*~~~

Week 3 Small Group Discussion Questions

(1) What has stood out to you or had the most impact on you in this week's study?

(2) In what ways do you see how the culture we live in has affected your relationships and how you view them?

(3) Romans 12:18 says, "Do all that you can to live in peace with everyone." Discuss this verse and how you have or could apply it to your relationships.

(4) How does seeing your ability to love the people in your life as a result of filling up on God's love instead of just trying harder affect you?

(5) How has unforgiveness damaged you in the past (or present)?

(6) What steps have you found helpful in learning to forgive?

(7) What is the most difficult thing about accepting the flaws and faults of those around you and loving them anyway?

(8) Discuss laying all of your relationships and loved ones on the altar at Jesus' feet.

Week 4
Situations and Circumstances

Section 1

I'm not sure if you've noticed, but we've been progressively moving from things that we have control over to things we don't.

While we have no control over other people and their decisions and behaviors, we can interact with them differently, which may have an effect on them and our relationships.

Often times, we have absolutely no control or influence on circumstances and situations in our lives.

Now granted, there are some circumstances and situations that are direct results of our decisions. But there are many that we have absolutely no say in.

I think of a friend's husband who was recently let go from his job after working for the same company for almost three decades. This reminds me of a friend's father who was placed in almost the same exact situation a few years ago.

I also think about a friend whose husband just died of a sudden massive stroke with absolutely no warning.

I think of the family who has a daughter with a severe genetic disorder that requires constant love and care.

The cousin who was diagnosed with terminal cancer at age 21.

The parents whose child started using drugs at age 12, unbeknownst to them, and was addicted by the time they had any hint anything was wrong.

The couple in our church who's house burned down in a random accident and lost everything.

The friend who was hit by another car and has had severe pain and effects of traumatic brain injury ever since.

Many women whose husbands chose to step outside of their marriage and have destroyed their families through cheating, lies, and deceit.

Men whose wives and mothers of their children just up and walked away.

The loved one who's trust and child were violated in unspeakable ways.

The list could go on and on of the situations and circumstances that people face every day. Things that are HARD.

Things that come with loads of stress.

You may think that I need to stop right here. That there's no way, given this list of things and all those left unspoken, that any one of us could live a stress-free life. That would be true, if we were talking about a life free of stressors.

But we're not.

We're talking about a life where we have been offered a great exchange. Not only has Jesus brought us from death to life, but He's offered us peace and joy for our stress, worry, and anxiety.

This sounds impossible, I know. Remember though, **nothing is impossible with God**. If we believe He can raise a dead, in the grave, starting to stink, body back to living, breathing, walking, talking, eating life, then we should have no problem believing He can bear all of our burdens and fill us with peace.

I feel like I need to say that again; NOTHING IS IMPOSSIBLE WITH GOD.

Not even bringing you peace in your most dire situation or anxiety-producing circumstance.

God's peace doesn't mean we don't have real feelings, that we don't hurt and cry and scream. It just means that in the midst of all of that we can still have peace and joy.

I'm reminded of the story of Horatio Spafford. You may not recognize his name, but I'm almost certain you'll recognize the title of his work: *It is Well*, the great hymn of reverence and complete trust in the Lord. If you haven't heard the story, I'll share the highlights, or lowlights as they may be, briefly. Spafford wrote this hymn after losing his four daughters on a ship that sank. AFTER losing his four daughters.

I cannot imagine this. Yet, I remember the words of my

friend's mom: our children (and anyone else in our lives) are not our own. They are the Lord's.

What great work the Lord must have done in Spafford's life to bring him to a place where his soul was at complete peace with God and life after this great tragedy.

He must have known full well the following verses.

> Peace I leave with you, my peace I
> give unto you: not as the world giveth,
> give I unto you. Let not your heart be
> troubled, neither let it be afraid.
> John 14:27 {KJV}

> I have told you all this so that you
> may have peace in me. Here on
> earth you will have many trials and
> sorrows. But take heart, because
> I have overcome the world.
> John 16:33

> Then you will experience God's
> peace, which exceeds anything
> we can understand. His peace
> will guard your hearts and minds
> as you live in Christ Jesus.
> Philippians 4:7

These verses are not meant to be platitudes. They are not meant to be posted on notes, pictures, and memorized just so we know them.

They are to be *engrained on our hearts* and *put into*

action.

Whenever we allow ourselves to be overcome by our situation or circumstance, we are not trusting God. We lack faith in what He is doing and question why He would allow this to happen.

Questioning why will never bring us peace. Neither will holding onto anxiety, worry, and stress.

Not only will they not bring us peace, nor allow us to have peace, they will brick by brick create a barrier between us and God.

If stress, anxiety, and worry are the opposite of faith and trust, then we are lacking faith when we choose them.

Read Hebrews 11:1-6.

This is the great chapter on faith. I love God's reminder that He is a rewarder of faith! Even faith as small as a mustard seed!! (see Matthew 17:20)

It is scary to think, though, if God rewards faith, what will He do in light of our lack of faith?

Before we move there, let's sit on a question you may have. Use the space below to write out Hebrews 11:1.

_____
_____
_____
_____

Faith is confidence. Confidence in what? According to this verse, that our hopes will come true. That we have assurance in God's promises even when we can't see them yet.

So, what's the question that may come up? It's this:

If God promises us what we hope for, why did _____ _____ (fill in the blank) happen?

Legitimate question. Wrong verse to use.

The pages before these verses on faith expound on God's new covenant with people based on Jesus' sacrificial death where He took on and swallowed the very wrath of the Lord.

The hope that's talked about here is our hope of salvation. We are confident in our being bought and brought into eternal life.

Read Hebrews 10:32-35

How powerfully these words are to speak into any difficulty! The Lord is so gracious. He knows we'll face trials. He fully understands this world we brought sin into. He is not surprised by any of it, as we often are. And He has provided encouragement after encouragement to trust in Him completely because He desires to infuse us with the very nature of His character.

He desires us to have peace.

He desires us to live full of joy.

He desires for our love to abound more and more. And all of this despite living in a fallen, dark, depraved world. Because of it, most likely. That we don't get too attached to the here and now and instead cling to the hope that we can be confident in – His faithful presence in us here and life in His presence for eternity.

~~~*~~~

Because of your faith, Christ has brought us into this place of undeserved privilege where we now stand, and we confidently and joyfully look forward to sharing in God's glory.
Romans 5:2

I pray that your hearts will be flooded with light so that you can understand the confident hope he has given to those he called – his holy people who are his rich and glorious inheritance.
Ephesians 1:18

My heart is confident in you, O God; my heart is confident. No wonder I can sing your praises!
Psalm 57:7

~~~*~~~

Section 2

I feel like the last section was a whirlwind. There was so much we covered and great concepts of faith and the Lord's desires and gifts for us.

Use the space below to record anything that touched you in a unique way or caught your attention anew:

_____

_____

_____

_____

It is amazing the great gifts God gives us. Gifts that are far greater than anything material.

> Now may the Lord of peace himself
> give you his peace at all times and in
> every situation. The Lord be with you all.
> 2 Thessalonians 3:16

The world tells us that peace comes from having the right spouse, job, house, toys, comforts, etc. Commercials abound with products promising peace. We are taught to pursue accomplishments, possessions, and all the good things in life we "deserve."

We are built up constantly for having the right things, experiences, and items. So, when we aren't able to have those things or experiences, when relationships fall apart, when jobs are lost, when tragedy strikes, our peace disappears faster than lightning.

There is a strong cultural connection between our circumstances and our level of peace.

Scripture, however, teaches us that peace is neither dependent on our situation nor should it be shaken by it.

How strongly would you say your peace is usually tied to your circumstances?

Loosely   Somewhat   Strongly

1   2   3   4   5   6   7   8   9   10

The only way for us to have peace and calm in the midst of the storms of life is if we cling to Jesus.

This doesn't, as I said before, mean we don't hurt and hurt deeply, it simply means we can continue to trust the Lord – and even praise Him – despite our trials and feelings.

Read through the following verses and underline every time "refuge" or "strength" shows up.

> But you are a tower of refuge to the poor, O Lord, a tower of refuge to the needy in distress. You are a refuge from the storm and a shelter from the heat. For the oppressive acts of ruthless people are like a storm beating against a wall....
> Isaiah 25:4

> This I declare about the LORD: He
> alone is my refuge, my place of safety;
> he is my God, and I trust him.
> Psalm 91:2

> God is our refuge and strength, always
> ready to help in times of trouble. So we
> will not fear when earthquakes come
> and the mountains crumble into the sea.
> Psalm 46:1-2

In reviewing these scriptures and looking back at 2 Thessalonians 3:16 (on the previous page) and John 16:33 (in yesterday's section), what conclusion do you make about how the connection between our peace and our circumstances?

_____

_____

_____

It's easy to say that we can have peace despite trials and tragedies, but how do we actually walk it out?

It all goes back to faith – trusting God completely.

I remember vividly when I once experienced this great contradiction. I was driving in my car alone, which doesn't happen very often, and my heart was extraordinarily heavy for a friend who was walking through a very difficult time. Tears poured down my face as my heart broke for this friend. Yet in the midst of my crying out to God for her pain, I was simultaneously able to rejoice in His greatness. I had perfect peace and tremendous pain all at the same time.

You may think this was because the pain wasn't directly mine, but if you've ever hurt with a friend, you'll know that's not the case.

Besides, there have been other trials I've walked through since then where my hurt was real and deep, yet my peace never left me. This particular experience was just the first time I really experienced keeping my peace despite my pain.

I've discovered the key to walking this out is to know God intimately. To have walked through a faith journey with Him where we've seen His faithfulness, lovingkindness, gentleness, protection, and sovereignty played out in great ways.

It's a decision, to dive into God's word and to spend time in prayer (both talking *and* listening), and choose to listen to *whatever* He's saying.

Unfortunately, in our world the secular culture is not the only influence that tells us that peace comes with things going our way. Many in the church have taken to espousing these ideas as well.

When we're taught to expect material blessings, favor, financial success, and all good things when we follow and obey God, it makes it that much harder to understand when trials and tragedies come.

The truth is sometimes God wipes away the storm and brings the blessings we desire. He also sometimes is the shelter that surrounds us as we hunker down and/or walk through the storm. He also allows storms to mold us, shape us, and make us more like Him.

Jesus told us that we would have troubles in this world (John 16:33). It is not an "if," it is a "when." Trials, heartaches, and sorrows are a part of life.

We can either focus on them, stress over them, lament over them, question them, and let them drag us down, or we can:

> ...run with endurance the race God has set before us. We do this by **keeping our eyes on Jesus**, the champion who initiates and perfects our faith....
> Hebrews 12:1b-2a
> {emphasis added}

It all goes back to the basics: reading the Word, spending time in prayer, and worshiping the Lord, Creator and Sustainer of the universe.

I hope you're not tired of me saying that yet. Because I might just say it again. Actually, I'm sure I'll say it again.

Whenever you try to change a behavior, thought pattern, or trait, it must be replaced with something else. Otherwise, it'll creep back in.

You may not believe stress and worry are behaviors, thought patterns, or traits, but they are learned. Sometimes we learn stress and anxiety from others in our lives, sometimes through experience.

And anything that's learned can be unlearned. Stress, anxiety, and worry are a ways of coping with trials, troubles, and tragedies that try to keep the control in our hands and have us trying to figure it all out.

Peace and joy, prayer and praise, faith and trust are ways of coping with the same exact things by admitting our lack of control and trusting God's sovereignty.

Nothing about the circumstances change, but our hearts and minds are dramatically different.

Have you ever experienced peace in a hard situation by turning to God? Share below.

_____

_____

_____

_____

Peace is possible in all circumstances! Remember, this doesn't mean we don't acknowledge real, hard feelings. It just means that we trust the One who will never disregard our feelings.

Use our closing time and the space below to pour out your heart to God about a situation or circumstance that is causing stress in your life. Turn it over to God. Ask Him to help you open your hand and let go of the grip you're trying to hold on it with. Seek His face and His peace and receive the gifts of His presence and Spirit.

_____

_____

_____

_____

~~~*~~~
Let all that I am wait quietly before God, for my hope I sin him. He alone is my rock and my salvation, my fortress where I will not be shaken. My victory and honor come from God alone. He is my refuge, a rock where no enemy can reach me. O my people, trust in him at all times. Pour out your heart to him, for God is our refuge.
Psalm 62:5-8
~~~*~~~

Section 3

Have you ever gotten that feeling in the pit of your stomach? You know the one, where it's all tied in knots. There's no peace and something inside you just won't settle down. It gnaws at you until you address it.

I've had this feeling more times than I care to admit. It's a physical manifestation of stress, this unease in your gut. Sometimes it's caused by situations and circumstances that are out of our control. Other times, though, it's caused by our own thoughts or actions.

When we've said or done something that leaves us unsettled. When we've left something unsaid or undone that ought to have been done.

This is a lack of peace due to sin.

Once again, God has taken us to a place unexpected. I'm not sure why I didn't realize ahead of time that He would take us here, but it caught me off guard a little.

The truth of the matter is, though, that sometimes our difficult circumstances and lack of peace are due to our own sin.

Sometimes it's because we've veered off the path of God's will.

Sometimes it's because we are not consistently in His word.

Sometimes it's because we're not in constant communication with Him.

Sometimes it's all of the above.

The truth is that we all fall short of God's perfect plan for us, even after we enter into a relationship with Him through faith in Jesus.

Every day I feel like I could be more obedient, more faithful, and more loving to the Lord.

It's not really in the success in accomplishing these things that eliminate my stress and bring me peace, but the pursuit of them. As long as our hearts are inclined to the Lord, He will give us peace in obedience and discontent in sin.

It's amazing how many verses there are about loving, meditating on, and following God's instructions and the benefits of doing so. Here are just a few:

> Those who love your instructions have
> great peace and do not stumble.
> Psalm 119:165

> The instructions of the LORD are
> perfect, reviving the soul. The
> decrees of the LORD are trustworthy,
> making wise the simple.
> Psalm 19:7

> Joyful are people of integrity, who
> follow the instructions of the LORD.
> Psalm 119:1

> I reflect at night on who you are, O
> LORD; therefore, I obey your instructions.
> Psalm 119:55

> O LORD, I have longed for your rescue,
> and your instructions are my delight.
> Psalm 119:174

The Lord has given us instructions not to limit us, control us, or to take away the joys of life, but to give us the best life possible. He has put boundaries around us to bring us joy and peace!

When we step outside of those boundaries, we step out of God's will and He will remove His peace from our hearts and lives in order to draw us back to Him.

Has there been a time in your life you've stepped out of God's will (big or small) and it stole your peace?

_____

_____

_____

I imagine the Lord was faithful to draw you back into His will. When you repented and reestablished your intimate fellowship with the Lord, did your peace return? Explain.

_____

_____

_____

_____

Now we come to the hard part. Is there something in your life currently that is keeping you from a peaceful communion with the Lord? Sin that has infiltrated your life and is robbing you of the gift of peace?

As you consider this question and pray over it, use the following scriptures to really open your heart to what the Lord might be correcting.

> Jesus replied, "The most important commandment is this: 'Listen O Israel! The LORD your God is the one and only LORD. And you must love the LORD your God with all your heart, all your soul, all your mind, and all your strength.' The second is equally important: 'Love your neighbor as yourself.' No other commandment is greater than these."
> Mark 12:29-31

> Their lives became full of every kind of wickedness, sin greed, , hate envy, murder, quarreling, deception, malicious behavior, and gossip. They are backstabbers, haters of God, insolent, proud, and boastful. They invent new ways of sinning, and they disobey their parents.
> Romans 1:29-30

> When you follow the desires of your sinful nature, the results are very clear: sexual immorality, impurity, lustful pleasures, idolatry, sorcery, hostility, quarreling, jealousy, outbursts of anger, selfish ambition, dissension, division, envy, drunkenness, wild parties, and other sins like these.
> Galatians 5:19-21a

I really hesitate to go here, because there is danger. First, there is danger in focusing on our sin and not on our Redeemer. Second, there is danger in glossing over these passages and patting ourselves on the back for not doing *that* bad. However, any close look at these passages on scripture will reveal the truth: we all fall short of God's perfection all the time.

In the church sins are often categorized. Some are viewed as horrendous, sending us to hell for eternity. Some are seen as struggles to overcome. Some aren't that big a deal.

I argue, however, from a biblical standpoint that every single sin is serious and separates us from the Lord. That's why He removes our peace when we sin.

I've even heard church members, brothers and sisters in Christ, laugh about sin. Like it's not really sin because it's accepted culturally.

However, no matter what level of seriousness we place on sin, gossip is just as much an affront to God as murder. Gluttony and lack of self-control are as offensive as homosexuality. Sex outside of marriage, drunkenness, lying, and stealing are all sins on the same level to God.

He is holy and anything short of us living holy lives is sin.

Let's take some time to really reflect on these verses (and any others God brings to mind). Splay open your heart and your life before a holy and perfect God and ask Him to purge anything within you or in your thoughts and behaviors that are keeping you from deep fellowship with Him and stealing your peace.

Use the lines below, if you're led, to write out your prayer.

_____

_____

_____

_____

_____

_____

_____

_____

_____

_____

~~~*~~~

Those who love your instructions have
great peace and do not stumble.
Psalm 119:165

Oh, what joy for those whose disobedience is forgiven, whose sin is put out of sight! Yes, what joy for those who record the Lord has cleared of guilt, whose lives are lived in complete honesty! When I refused to confess my sin, my body wasted away and I groaned all day long. Day and night your hand of discipline was heavy on me. My strength evaporated like water in the summer heat. Finally, I confessed all my sins to you and stopped trying to hide my guilt. I said to myself, "I will confess my rebellion to the Lord." And you forgave me! All my guilt is gone.
Psalm 32:1-5

~~~*~~~

Section 4

As we come so very close to finishing out our time together in studying how to live stress-free, there is one a piece of the puzzle that's been hinted at, but not really talked about.

Faith in God – in who He is and the reality of His promises – is a major key to eliminating stress, worry, and anxiety in our lives and cope with stressors. While faith may not seem very active, like it's something we can actually *do*, it is.

> Faith is the confidence that what we
> hope for will actually happen; it gives us
> assurance about things we cannot see.
> Hebrews 11:1

Our confidence is in the Lord's promises, His character, and His word. We can choose to stand on and believe what He says and seek Him through prayer.

There's another aspect here, too, that's absolutely essential to peaceful living: worship.

I read a great quote the other day that fits perfectly with this study and this truth.

> "Worship gets you through the hardest times in your life because it shifts your focus from the problem to the problem solver."

It was then followed by this elaboration: "When you can't change your situation, you can change your perspective." {*To Save a Life* Facebook Page 5/15/15}

If you're looking for something to *do* instead of stress and worry, look no further.

Diving into, studying, and meditating on scripture is immeasurably helpful. God will speak to your mind and heart and remind you of His greatness. He will use His word to change your thoughts, just as we're told in Romans.

> Don't copy the behavior and customs of
> this world, but let God transform you into a
> new person by changing the way you think.
> Then you will learn to know God's will for you,
> which is good and pleasing and perfect.
> Romans 12:2

In addition to diving into the word, we can also spend time in communication with the Lord through prayer. This will fill your soul up.

> Pray in the Spirit at all times and
> on every occasion. Stay alert
> and be persistent in your prayers
> for all believers everywhere.
> Ephesians 6:18-19

However, the act of worshiping the Lord and Creator of the universe is an action that gives us something to do, draws us closer to Him, and will pull us out of negative thought cycles.

I love the last verses of Psalms 42 and 43 that show this truth. After lamenting grief, despair, and discouragement, the author ends with the answer to stress: praise.

> Why am I discouraged? Why is my
> heart so sad? I will put my hope
> in God! I will praise him again
> –my Savior and my God!
> Psalm 42:11 ~ Psalm 42:5

We also see the importance of worship and praise in various other areas. Read these two examples and circle every word that has to do with praising the Lord.

> Honor the LORD for the glory of
> his name. Worship the LORD in
> the splendor of his holiness.
> Psalm 29:2

> Come, let us worship and bow down.
> Let us kneel before the LORD our
> maker, for he is our God. We are
> the people he watches over, the
> flock under his care. If only you
> would listen to his voice today!
> Psalm 95:6-7

There is nothing quite like worshiping God in the midst of a storm. It's one thing to worship him when everything's going okay. It's a whole other level of experience of communion with the Lord when we worship Him in our distress.

Have you ever experienced God's renewing of your heart and mind through worship in a difficult time?

_____

_____

What do you think makes the difference between Bible reading and prayer alone, and bible reading and prayer with worship added?

_____

_____

_____

Praise seems to multiply our time with God. It takes us to a deeper, more intimate fellowship with Him. This is true most likely because He was made to be worshiped and we were made to worship.

Read Psalm 148:1-5 and use the lines below to write out verse 5.

_____

_____

_____

_____

What reason does this verse give for our reason to praise the Lord?

_____

We are His! He created us. There's nothing any one of us can do to bring ourselves into being, make ourselves keep breathing, or living. We are sustained in this life only due to the sovereignty and power of God.

When we worship, we not only give God His due, but we bring unity between our flesh and the Spirit that indwells us.

> Don't you realize that your body is the temple of the Holy Spirit, who lives in you and was given to you by God? You do not belong to yourself, for God bought you with a high price. So you must honor God with your body.
> 1 Corinthians 6:19-20

These verses are referring to keeping our bodies from sexual sin, but they also reveal a deeper truth that we know but don't often meditate on: that God's Spirit *dwells in us.*

So when we worship God with our mouths and bodies, we bring our body and spirit into unity – and are filled with peace.

Isn't that an amazing reality?

As we close, I'd like to use this time to praise the Lord. Maybe spend time in the Word seeking out promises and characteristics of God that reveal to us His great worthiness of being praised. Maybe list the things you're grateful for. Maybe just put on some praise music and sing as loud as you can. However God is calling you to praise His name, spend that time now as we close.

Then, if you desire, use the space below to write a prayer or record your experience.

_____

_____

_____

~~~*~~~
All praise to God, the Father of our
Lord Jesus Christ, who has blessed
us with every spiritual blessing
in the heavenly realms because
we are united with Christ.
Ephesians 1:3
~~~*~~~

Section 5

I think this is the hardest part of the Bible study I've written yet. Probably because I know it's the last section and the study is coming to an end. I hope that you have been blessed and would love to know if you have! (see the last pages for ways to contact me and let me know how this Bible study has impacted our life.)

I wonder, really, if there's anything left to say. There must be, because God in His sovereignty brought us here.

We could recap everything that we've learned, and really that's my inclination. If you're anything like me, you love diving into a good book or Bible study and love the truths within it, but forget much of it when you move on to the next thing.

You have this book, though, to reread, study, or use as a reference any time you desire.

Besides, it doesn't feel like the Spirit is leading us to go backwards, but forward.

That's the whole point – to leave not the same as we began, but changed. Hopefully you, like me, have been molded to be a little more like Christ. You've looked into some hard things and laid them before the Lord. You've drawn closer to and gotten to know Him more.

We want to use any opportunity to allow the Holy Spirit to continue to mature us.

While we desire for life to be stress-free in the sense of everything going our way, the Lord allows – and gasp!

sometimes even brings – trials our way to help make us more like Him.

When we choose stress, anxiety, and worry, we stay babes in faith and hinder our own faith walk. When we choose faith, drawing closer to the Lord and worshiping Him, we take a step towards being complete in Him.

> Dear brothers and sisters, when
> troubles of any kind come your way,
> consider it an opportunity for great joy.
> For you know that when your faith is
> tested, your endurance has a chance
> to grow. So let it grow, for when
> your endurance is fully developed,
> you will be perfect and
> complete, needing nothing.
> James 1:2-4

This life is a journey and our faith life is a journey. We won't reach that perfection until we're in heaven with the Lord, but we can certainly move closer and closer to it.

Look up and write out 2 Corinthians 3:18.

_____

_____

_____

_____

_____

_____

God desires to change us for a purpose: to become more like Him.

So, whether our stress is from our schedules, relationships, or circumstances, whether it's something God ordained or simply allowed, the goal is the same.

No matter how small or big the issue, we have the same opportunity to either:

(1) stress and worry and build a barrier between us and God.

or

(2) trust God and live in His supernatural peace and draw closer to and become more like Him.

Each day we have the opportunity to choose. It won't always be easy. It won't always be simple. But with God, it is possible to live a stress-free, joy-and-peace-filled life.

~~~*~~~

Keep putting into practice all you
learned and received from me – everything
you heard from me and saw me doing.
Then the God of peace will be with you.
Philippians 4:9

Rather, you must grow in the grace
knowledge of our Lord and Savior
Jesus Christ. All glory to him, both
now and forever! Amen.
2 Peter 3:18

~~~*~~~

Week 4 Small Group Discussion Questions

(1) Discuss the hope we have in the Lord and how it changes your perspective.

(2) How does it feel to hear that stress, anxiety, and worry are the opposite of faith in God?

(3) How can you make God your refuge in any and every storm of life?

(4) What (if anything) in your background has taught you that peace and joy are dependent on circumstances?

(5) How was examining sin in your life that might be robbing you of your peace with and from God?

(6) How does adding worship and praise affect your ability to live in the Lord's peace?

(7) Discuss God using stressors and trials to draw us closer to and mold us to be more like Him.

(8) How can you both put the biblical truths found in this study into practice in your life and pass them along to others in your life?

About the Author

I am a lover of Jesus who is amazed at not only how He reveals Himself day-to-day, but also the greater understanding He gives me as I continue pursuing Him and His truth. I had no idea He'd ever call me to write and speak to feed the lessons He teaches me into the lives of other women. Certainly, I never expected I'd be writing Bible studies. Doing so is a walk of obedience in my trembling socked feet. I want everything I say and write to honor the Lord and know how imperfect I am and that I'll get things wrong. This makes me want to shrink back from this calling. But I've learned the freedom and joy in walking in obedience to the Lord, so I forge ahead.

In addition to being a woman humbled by her call into ministry for the Lord and Creator of the universe, I am also a wife and mother of four beautiful children. I've been blessed to be a stay-at-home mom since child #2 was born and homeschooling mom for almost a decade. These jobs keep me busy, but also allow me to fulfill the call God's placed on my life.

I love connecting with other women. Since I know we can't all meet for coffee, I'd love to connect with you online. Use any or all of the means below to share your feedback with me on this study. Or to ask questions. Or to just say hi.

I pray the Lord has blessed you and will continue to do so with the greatest gifts He has to offer as you walk closer and closer to Him and allow yourself to be #transformed by His #grace.

Tracy Wainwright

www.tracywainwright.com
Email: tracy_wainwright@yahoo.com
Facebook: Tracy Wainwright Author Page
Twitter: @TracyWrites4Him
Instagram: TracyLWainwright
More about the Abundant Life Conference for Women:
www.abundantlifeconferenceforwomen.com

www.ingramcontent.com/pod-product-compliance
Lightning Source LLC
LaVergne TN
LVHW052254070426
835507LV00035B/2895